P9-CFM-981

1 2 3 4 5 6 7

100

90

80

70

60

50

40 30 20 15 14 13

8

9

10

11

12

One Nation

America by the Numbers

Written by Devin Scillian
Illustrated by Pam Carroll

Text Copyright © 2002 Devin Scillian
Illustration Copyright © 2002 Pam Carroll

All rights reserved. No part of this book may be reproduced in any manner
without the express written consent of the publisher, except in the case of brief
excerpts in critical reviews and articles. All inquiries should be addressed to:

Sleeping Bear Press
310 North Main Street
P.O. Box 20
Chelsea, MI 48118
www.sleepingbearpress.com
1 800 487-2323

Printed and bound in Canada.

10 9 8 7 6 5 4 3 2

Library of Congress Cataloging-in-Publication Data
Scillian, Devin
One nation : America by the numbers / by Devin Scillian ; illustrated
by Pam Carroll.
p. cm.
Summary: A counting book presenting various aspects of the United States, from
the concept of one nation to the hundred men and women in the U.S. Senate.
ISBN: 1-58536-063-5
1. United States-Miscellanea-Juvenile literature. 2. Counting-Juvenile literature.
3. United States-Miscellanea-Juvenile literature. 4. Counting-Juvenile literature.
[1. United States-Miscellanea. 2. Counting.] I. Carroll, Pamela, ill. II. Title.

E178.3.S335 2002
973—dc21   2002021698

For Troy, my younger brother and oldest friend.

D.S.

I dedicate this book to the unsung heroes of education. To Elizabeth Adams, Kathy Wood, and Beth Jauregui, fine teachers dedicated to the principle that a child's potential is always greater than his or her performance. To my husband Chris and my son Dustin, thank you for keeping the vision alive. Finally, I wish to dedicate this book to the children of America: Follow your dreams and never waiver, for the best is yet to come!

P.C.

The United States of America are 50 states with thousands of cities and millions of people. But together they make 1 nation. The U.S.A. is like a great patchwork quilt, sewn over the years by people who came to our shores from all over the world, bringing with them many customs, cultures, and even languages. All of those people and traditions come together in a special way that makes the United States a country like no other.

Americans promise to be loyal to their country in the Pledge of Allegiance, written by Francis Bellamy in 1892:

I pledge allegiance to the flag of the United States of America, and to the Republic for which it stands, one nation, under God, indivisible, with liberty and justice for all.

Mm Nn Oo Pp Qq Rr Ss Tt Uu Vv Ww
'6 17 18/9 20

giance ✗

to the flag
es of America
r which it
er God,
ty and Justice

Homework :

1. Learn your numbers

ONE
one

D.C.

Franklin

Pip

Lu Lu

George and Martha

Stuart

A number of things are on my mind.
    They're each red, white, and blue.
You count on me, America,
    and today I'm counting on you.

One nation, under God, indivisible,
    with liberty and justice for all.

One of each, just like your shoes,
America sometimes comes in **twos**.
Two for South, **two** for North,
Carolinas and Dakotas, back and forth.
Two big neighbors stuck like glue,
Mexico, **one**, and Canada, **two**.

North Carolina and South Carolina are in the southeastern United States. Both of the Carolinas were among the 13 original colonies.

North Dakota and South Dakota are in the northern United States. Before becoming states, both North and South Dakota were part of the Dakota Territory. Those living in the territory couldn't agree on a capital city, so Congress divided the territory into two states, North Dakota and South Dakota.

The United States, Mexico, and Canada are the three nations that make up the continent of North America.

2

The *Niña*, the *Pinta*, and the *Santa Maria* were the 3 ships brought to the new world by Christopher Columbus in 1492. Together, the 3 ships carried almost 100 men.

When our nation was brand new, many Americans wore 3-cornered hats, also known as tricorn hats.

The minutemen were soldiers who helped our nation win its independence from Great Britain. They had to be ready to move with just a minute's notice, so they were called minutemen.

I count to **three** just like that.
I count the corners on my hat.
A **three**-cornered hat from a Boston store,
one just like the minutemen wore.
Or count the ships. There's an idea,
the *Niña*, the *Pinta*, and *Santa Maria*.

Mt. Rushmore is in the Black Hills of South Dakota. It's an enormous granite sculpture of 4 of our greatest presidents. Gutzon Borglum started carving the sculpture in 1927 and worked on it until he died in 1941. His son, Lincoln Borglum, oversaw the final work on the sculpture. If the heads on Mt. Rushmore had matching bodies, each man would be nearly 500 feet tall.

4

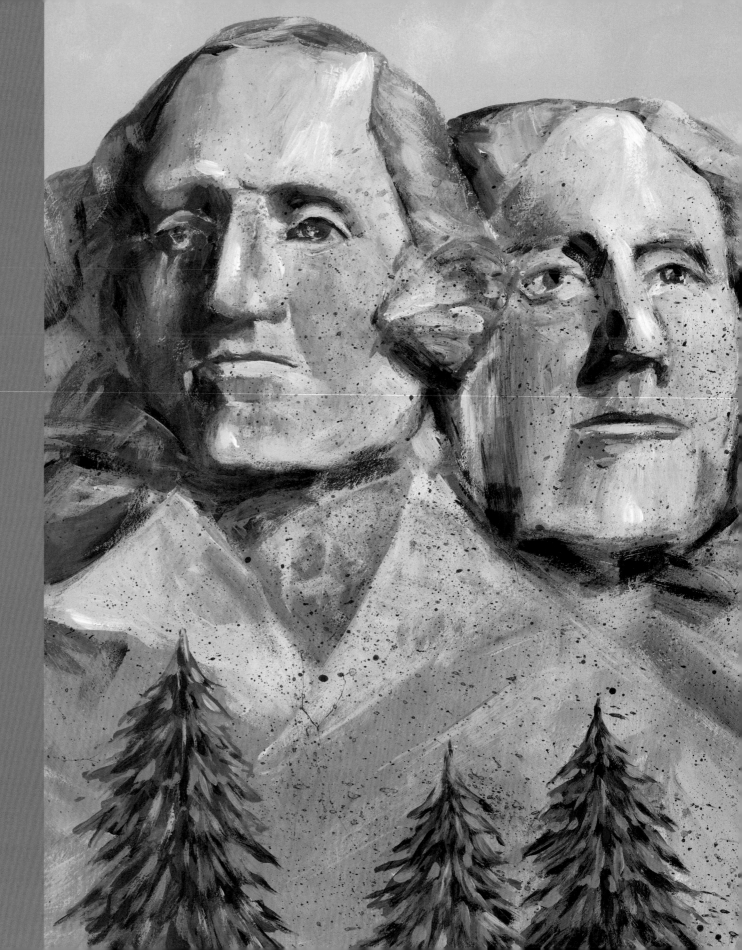

A massive way to count to **four**,
the **four** great men on Mt. Rushmore.
We'll start with George Washington, one,
Jefferson, two. We're halfway done.
Roosevelt, three, and just one more—
Abraham Lincoln makes it **four**.

The five Great Lakes make up the largest system of fresh water on earth.

The water that pours over Niagara Falls is on a long journey toward the Atlantic Ocean. One way to remember the Great Lakes is to remember the word "HOMES."

H for Huron
O for Ontario
M for Michigan
E for Erie and
S for Superior.

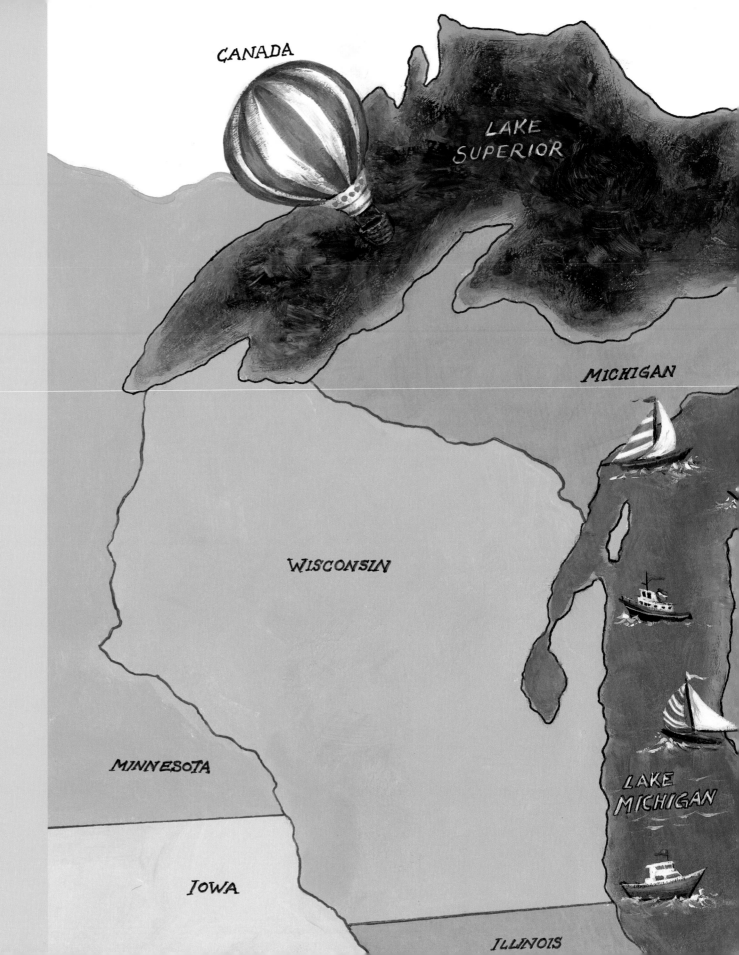

CANADA

LAKE SUPERIOR

MICHIGAN

WISCONSIN

MINNESOTA

LAKE MICHIGAN

IOWA

ILLINOIS

To count to **five** it merely takes
a trip along the **five** Great Lakes.
Superior deep and Michigan blue,
Huron leads to the other two.
Ontario answers when Erie calls
over the roar of Niagara Falls.

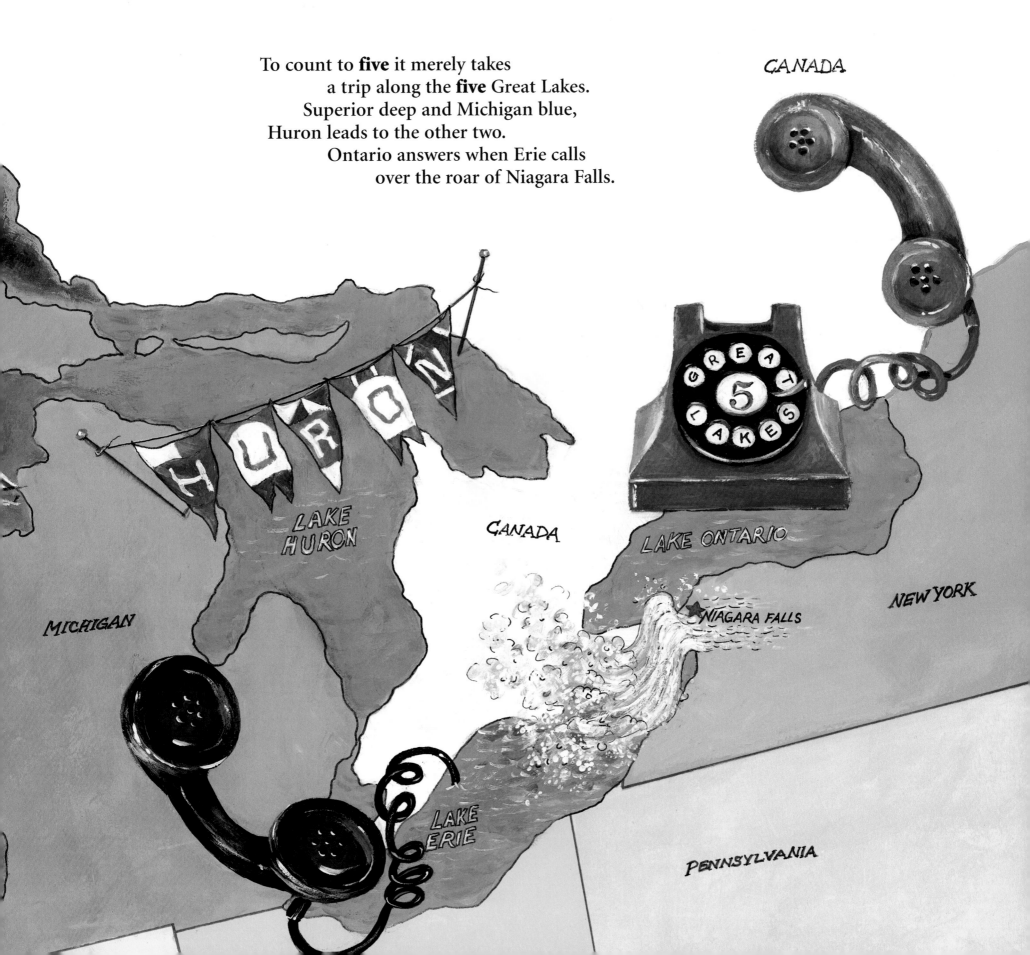

To count to **six** you need to stand
as far northeast as you can.
The New England states are perfect picks.
Count them all and you'll find **six**.
And maple syrup from trees so tall—
they paint New England every fall.

The New England states are Maine, Vermont, Connecticut, Rhode Island, Massachusetts, and New Hampshire. Like the Pilgrims who came to Plymouth, Massachusetts, many of the first European settlers to arrive in North America came to New England.

Captain John Smith named the region when he explored its shores in 1614 for some London merchants.

Many people travel to New England in the autumn to see the beautiful colors of the changing leaves. New England is famous for delicious seafood such as lobster and clams.

6

We look to the sky, we look toward heaven
and count our way through the Mercury **Seven**.
Seven pioneers, **seven** brave men—
Carpenter, Cooper, Grissom, and Glenn.
Schirra, Shepard, and Slayton each knew
that our future lay beyond the blue.

The Mercury Seven were the nation's first astronauts. Over 500 pilots were considered for the United States space program. But the lucky 7 were chosen and announced in 1959. They were:

M. Scott Carpenter
L. Gordon Cooper Jr.
Virgil I. "Gus" Grissom
John H. Glenn Jr.
Walter M. Schirra Jr.
Alan B. Shepard Jr.
Donald K. "Deke" Slayton

From this group, Alan Shepard was chosen to be the first American to fly into space. The suborbital flight lasted 15½ minutes. John Glenn, on a later mission, was the first American to orbit the earth. His flight lasted 4 hours and 55 minutes.

7

More states begin with the letter "M" than any other letter. Each of the M states is associated with water. Mississippi and Missouri are not only states; they are also the names of very important American rivers. Montana is known as the Headwaters State because much of the water that flows to the rest of the country comes from the mountains of Montana. It is the only state in the Union from which waters flow to the Hudson Bay, the Gulf of Mexico, and the Pacific Ocean. Water is also important in Minnesota, which has thousands of lakes. And Michigan, Maine, Maryland, and Massachusetts have thousands of miles of coastline.

8

1. Montana
2. Massachusetts
3. Maryland
4. Missouri
5. Mississippi
6. Minnesota
7. Michigan
8. Maine

states that start with M ⑧

$$\begin{array}{r} 6 \\ +2 \\ \hline 8 \end{array}$$

$2 \times 4 = 8$

Hi

On to **eight** and even better,
we'll take our number and add a letter.
Montana, Massachusetts, and Maryland, too.
Missouri, Mississippi, and Minnesota will do.
Add Michigan and Maine. Isn't that great?
The M states help us count to **eight**.

$$\begin{array}{r} 4 \\ +4 \\ \hline 8 \end{array}$$

A baseball team needs 3 outfielders, 4 infielders, a pitcher, and a catcher. Baseball is played all over America, from Little League parks to the World Series that is held every October.

The most important legal decisions in our country are made by the Supreme Court. The 9 Supreme Court justices are appointed by the president. Once a justice is appointed to the Supreme Court, he or she can be a Supreme Court justice for life.

Out on a diamond in a summertime shine,
    a baseball team will give us **nine**.
        A game that's filled with American pride,
    it takes **nine** players to play for each side.
Or let's find **nine** of a different sort—
        the number of judges on our Supreme Court.

9

The first leaders of our young nation created the Constitution to guide our government. But some believed that it needed something more. They believed the rights of all Americans should be plainly written down for all to see. That list of 10 amendments is known as the Bill of Rights. The amendments were drafted by James Madison who would later become our 4th president.

10

To count to **ten** just set your sights
on what we call the Bill of Rights.
Our founding fathers thought to leave
a list of all that we believe.
Ten amendments making clear
the rights and freedoms we hold dear.

One more than ten, four more than seven,
we just head south to find **eleven**.
The Dixie states, the land of peaches,
country hams, and southern beaches.
Growing peanuts by the ton—
eleven states in the Dixie sun.

The Dixie states are Virginia, North Carolina, South Carolina, Georgia, Alabama, Tennessee, Texas, Mississippi, Arkansas, Louisiana, and Florida.

The U.S.A. gets a lot of its food from the farms and orchards of the South, such as oranges and grapefruit from Florida. The South is famous for many kinds of American music, from the jazz of New Orleans, to the blues of Memphis, to the country music of Nashville.

The state of Virginia has produced 8 presidents. In fact, 4 of the nation's first 5 presidents came from Virginia.

11

Your mom, your brother, your uncle, your cousin;
we all buy lots of things by the dozen.
A dozen is **twelve** for sale in a store—
doughnuts and eggs and roses and more.
Remember as you stand at the grocery shelves,
when you buy by the dozen, you're buying in **twelves**.

We use 12 in many different ways in everyday life. There are a dozen inches in a foot, and 3 dozen inches in a yard. There are 2 dozen hours in a day, and a dozen months in a year. In American courtrooms, a jury is often made up of 12 people.

Sometimes things, such as bagels, are sold as a baker's dozen, which means 13 instead of 12.

12

Thirteen stripes in white and red
on the American flag overhead.
Why **thirteen**? It just makes sense,
for each bright stripe represents
one of the proud, original few.
From **thirteen** states our nation grew.

There are 13 stripes on the American flag—7 red and 6 white. Betsy Ross is believed to have sewn the first American flag in 1776. The first flag had not only 13 stripes, but 13 stars as well. As states were added to the Union, stars were added to the flag. American flags are flown all over the country, but there is also an American flag on the moon and one on Mt. Everest, the highest peak in the world.

13

Both New York and New Hampshire at one time claimed Vermont belonged to them. And for a while, Britain thought about making Vermont a part of Canada. But Vermont was an independent republic when it joined the United States in 1791. In 1794 the flag changed from 13 to 15 stars, adding both Vermont and Kentucky.

14

Everyone knows of the first thirteen, but think of what came later—
a brand new state, the first of many, to make our nation greater.
You'll find **fourteen** on Lake Champlain, beyond a beautiful ridge,

in a white birch forest by a country church beside a covered bridge.
Thirty-seven times, we added a state, each cause for celebration.
So let's salute lovely Vermont, the **fourteenth** state in the nation.

For **fifteen** years, they drew up their plans,
constructed her torch and polished her hands.
They built her, then broke her, then placed her in crates,
and shipped her from France to the United States.
It took **fifteen** years, but she stands there today,
Our Lady of Liberty, lighting the way.

The Statue of Liberty was a gift from the people of France, where it was designed and created. It was then broken down into 350 pieces and in 1885 it was shipped to the United States in 214 crates. Like a giant puzzle, it arrived in New York and was put back together. In 1886, Lady Liberty made her appearance in New York Harbor and became a symbol of freedom for people all over the world.

15

To count to **twenty** I hope you're thinkin'
of Honest Abe, Abraham Lincoln.
Long ago, in the Civil War,
the number **twenty** was called a "score."
The Gettysburg Address began just so:
"Four score and seven years ago..."

A score is 20, so when Abraham Lincoln said "Four score and seven years," he meant 87 years.

The Gettysburg Address is a speech President Lincoln gave in Gettysburg, Pennsylvania, in 1863 during the Civil War. It was a short speech; it contains only 272 words and probably lasted just 2 or 3 minutes. But it remains one of the most famous speeches in American history.

20

Isn't it something? Isn't it nifty
that the states add up to exactly **fifty**?
As our nation grew, we had to wait.
It seemed we were stuck on forty-eight.
Alaska and Hawaii, one large and one small,
made **fifty** United States in all.

The oldest states in the nation have been part of the United States since 1776. The youngest states, Alaska and Hawaii, joined the Union 183 years later in 1959, and are the only states not attached to the continental U.S. Alaska is the nation's largest state. Rhode Island is the nation's smallest state. More people live in California than any other state. Wyoming has the smallest population of any state.

50

Greetings from Hawaii

★ HONOLULU

50

★ SALT LAKE CITY
UTAH 45

★ SANTA FE
NEW MEXICO

★ OKLAHOMA CITY
OKLAHOMA 46

47

PHOENIX ★
ARIZONA 48

50

To reach **one hundred**, here's the U.S. Senate
with **one hundred** men and women in it.
A pair from each state and, of course, you knew
that makes **one hundred**—fifty times two.
If that doesn't remind you, Ben Franklin will.
He's on the **one hundred** dollar bill.

100

THE UNITED STATES OF AMERICA

100

On and on, we could count all day
and count each person in the U.S.A.
For that's what counts the most, you know,
the people who make our country go.
The United States, the land of the free,
I've counted on you and you can count on me.

ONE HUNDRED DOLLARS

The United States Congress makes the laws of the United States. Congress is divided into 2 parts, the Senate and the House of Representatives. Each state has 2 senators, but the number of representatives depends on the state's population.

Born in 1706, Ben Franklin was a scientist, an inventor, a statesman, a philosopher, and one of America's greatest citizens. Pictured on the back of the 100-dollar bill, you'll find Independence Hall where Ben Franklin worked for American independence.

100

Devin Scillian

For Devin Scillian, the number **4** comes in particularly handy. He and his wife Corey have **4** children (Griffin, Quinn, Madison, and Christian). He manages to juggle **4** occupations (journalist, author, musician, and songwriter). And each night, he anchors the news for Channel **4**, WDIV-TV, the NBC affiliate in Detroit. He and his family live in Grosse Pointe Park, Michigan.

His other books include *A is for America: An American Alphabet* (also illustrated by Pam Carroll) and *Fibblestax*, illustrated by Kathryn Darnell.

Pam Carroll

California native Pam Carroll was a finalist in *Artist's Magazine*'s Still Life category for the past two years. Her distinct style of realism and appealing use of light creates an enchanting visual experience for children. In addition to *One Nation*, Pam has also illustrated *A is for America: An American Alphabet*; *S is for Star: A Christmas Alphabet*; and *G is for Golden: A California Alphabet*. She lives with her husband Chris, in Carmel, California, where she paints daily. She is an active member of the Carmel Art Association and the Hauk Fine Art Gallery in Pacific Grove.